Dr. Frances Meritt Stern is Director of the Institute for Behavioral Awareness, a consulting and counseling center in New Jersey. Her expertise has been effectively employed with businesses, national groups, private clients, and community organizations. **Rom Zemke** is research editor for *Training, the Magazine of Human Resource Development*, and is a training consultant in the Minneapolis-St. Paul area. In addition he has been a University of Minnesota Research Fellow specializing in instructional psychology, personal growth, and motivation systems.

Frances Meritt Stern
Ron Zemke

Stress-less Selling

a guide to success for men & women in sales

A SPECTRUM BOOK

PRENTICE-HALL, INC., Englewood Cliffs, New Jersey 07632

Library of Congress Cataloging in Publication Data

Stern, Frances Meritt (date)
  Stressless selling.

  (A Spectrum Book)
  Bibliography: p.
  Includes index.
  1. Sales Personnel. 2. Job stress. I. Zemke,
Ron, joint author. II. Title.
HF5439.5.S73   658.8'5   80-23419
ISBN 0-13-852749-0
ISBN 0-13-852731-8 (pbk.)

Interior design by Dawn L. Stanley
Cover design by Tony Ferrara Studio, Inc.
Manufacturing buyer: Cathie Lenard

A SPECTRUM BOOK

10 9 8 7 6 5 4 3 2 1

Printed in the United States of America

PRENTICE-HALL INTERNATIONAL, INC., *London*
PRENTICE-HALL OF AUSTRALIA PTY. LIMITED, *Sydney*
PRENTICE-HALL OF CANADA, LTD., *Toronto*
PRENTICE-HALL OF INDIA PRIVATE LIMITED, *New Delhi*
PRENTICE-HALL OF JAPAN, INC., *Tokyo*
PRENTICE-HALL OF SOUTHEAST ASIA PTE. LTD., *Singapore*
WHITEHALL BOOKS LIMITED, *Wellington, New Zealand*

contents

APPENDIXES 261

preface

It's a fact that all of us experience stress. It can be *constructive* stress, such as the positive, mobilizing, energizing stress a speaker experiences before speaking or an athlete before competing. Or it can be *negative,* immobilizing stress — an unexpected, nasty retort from a prospect or a sudden skid on a patch of ice — that can cause us to panic and momentarily "freeze up." Sometimes the stress we encounter leads us to experience strain or tension that is short-lived and mild. And that's fine, because it adds excitement and pleasure to what we do. Some event (or series of events), the anticipation of an event, even the mental re-living of a past event seem to trigger a temporary anxious or nervous reaction — a sort of tension or disquiet. At other times, we experience severe, debilitating stress that seems to build slowly and go on forever. It can disrupt our ability to concentrate, create, problem solve, eat, sleep, laugh, love, and generally enjoy life in its most whole, robust, and rewarding forms. And it happens to the best of us.

As Alvin Toffler, author of *Future Shock,* and others suggest, the ever-increasing rate of change of civilization, technology and lifestyle have taxed our innate abilities to cope, to change with change and to go on about the business of becoming who and how we want to be, accomplishing what we want to accomplish. Maybe. Maybe not. Whatever the case, it's unquestionably true today that many people find their "wired-in" coping skills taxed. It's equally true that many people have succeeded in bringing order and joy back into their lives by using the techniques, ideas, skills, philosophies, and "tips and tricks" you'll find in this book.

Some of these tools are as old as the hills — but as good as gold. Others are disarmingly simple. Some are a touch esoteric and a few are, quite frankly, experimental. All of them have track records of success when used in the right stiuation, at the right time, in the right way. It's our goal to help you find the right way(s) to manage and minimize, orchestrate and control, the stress in your unique life so that you can get on about the real business of life — becoming who you want to become.

HOW TO USE THIS BOOK

This book is a combination of things. In part, it is a book you can sit and read. In part, it is a set of ideas and research findings for you to test yourself against. It is also a catalogue of carefully constructed stress-management exercises, techniques, and strategies you will learn and use.

The book is divided into three sections.

Section I contains 12 chapters. Chapter 1 is a brief examination of the history of stress as an important work and life problem. Chapters 2 through 12 are short and to-the-point and deal solely with the stress issues that face the sales professional. The content comes from our separate consulting practices and our joint and separate research efforts. Use the ten self-tests in these Section I chapters to measure the degree to which each of the stress issues discussed affects you personally. Incidentally, these self-tests are more than diversions and curiosity satisfiers. They are carefully constructed and tested inventories that we will show you how to use for diagnosing your personal stress problems.

In Section II, you will combine the results of the Section I self-tests with the results of three more stress inventories. We will show you how to use these results to build your *Personal Stress Profile* and to develop one or more *Stress Management Prescriptions* for managing your unique stresses.

In Section III, we will discuss stress treatment and introduce several stress management strategies. You will probably never read all of them. You can if you like, but the step-by-step how-to strategies in Section III are designed to address the unique stress management needs you pinpointed in Section II.

Obviously, no individual would ever need *all* the techniques in Section III.

During the developmental testing of this book, a few of our readers questioned the logic of holding the "solutions" until Section III. But our decision to do so was not an arbitrary one. Our view is that stress is not a simple problem with easy solutions. Stress is a many-sided issue, and to effectively manage it, you must understand the "nature of the beast." In fact, we feel that developing this *awareness* is an important part of your management efforts. It is also important, in our view, that *you* see your entire stress profile and *you* take an active part in both developing the diagnosis and building the treatment plan. It's your life and taking a proactive approach to solving your life problems is also an important part of stress management. That's why the structure of the book is:

Section   I   — Information

Section II   — Diagnosis

Section III   — Treatment

Our work with professional salespeople has taught us a lot. We are impressed with the creative, intelligent way they approach their profession and with the sophisticated coping skills many have developed on their own for managing the stresses of selling for a living. We have also found that even the sales pros with good stress-management skills are eager to add additional skills to their repertoires. We believe that the awareness and the new skills to be gained from reading this book and working through the exercises and practices will greatly increase that store of knowledge. Furthermore, we believe that these skills will help you free extra energy. Energy you can use for selling. Energy you can use for living better and more fully. Energy you can use for achieving your true success potential.

ACKNOWLEDGEMENTS

This book is a distillation of five years' experience with the stress issues faced by professional salespeople. We have worked with and learned from both neophytes and highly successful, seasoned veterans. We thank them all.

We are particularly indebted to the following sales professionals for their very specific contributions: The analytical Sid Isler who spent long hours nitpicking over the manuscript; Norman W. Kamerow, CLU, a cerebral, effective sales professional who provided his special insights, and Frank Ward, who provided the perspective of a gifted salesman/sales manager. In addition, we thank Jane M. Shiff, CLU, who willingly shared her expertise in working with women in sales; Chester R. Jones, CLU, who helped us with the tone and feel of the manuscript; and Susan Jones, who brought her special wordsmithing skills to our aid. We are also indebted to Dorothea R. Johnson, MD, Medical Director AT&T Long Lines, for her feedback and professional input.

Finally, we'd like to thank our respective staffs for their aid and forbearance. Among them, special thanks are due Muriel Klinger, for her seminal contributions to the project concepts, and to Audrey Kupers, for her dedication to excellence.

Frances Meritt Stern, Ph.D.
Director, Institute for Behavioral Awareness
Springfield, New Jersey

Ron Zemke
Performance Research Associates
Minneapolis, Minnesota

introduction
and overview

Stress is one of those "you-know-it-when-you-have-it-but-it's-hard-to-explain-it-to-someone-else" concepts similar to fear, fatigue, or love. This definition problem will be tackled shortly, because it's crucial that we agree on what we're talking about. For now, let's look at the forest and save the individual trees till later.

Have you ever been so worried about something in your personal or professional life that you paced about, thinking and rethinking a situation until every other aspect of your life seemed secondary and unimportant? How did all that worrying affect you? Your life? The people around you? Did you develop the shakes? Sweaty palms? Catch yourself biting your nails? Were you constantly tired and weary but unable to sleep? Did you lose your appetite? Drink a bit too much? Kick the cat and holler at the kids? Trample on the sensitivities of kith, kin, and colleagues?

And, finally, when you think back, did any of that preoccupation, sweating, nail-biting, hollering, and hiding *solve the problem* you were worrying about? No, of course not. You wasted a lot of energy on unproductive activities that got in the way of everything you wanted to be doing. The problem, when it was solved, was solved by—what else?—*solving the problem*. Some may argue that the stress energized you to solve the problem. And that *can* and *does* happen. But most of us lack the skills necessary to manage and use *severe* stress in a positive fashion. Most of us move directly from motivated to "tilt" and only take hold of the problem *after* the stress has subsided, *after* precious time and energy have burned away in dysfunctional worry and anguish.

Interrupting that cycle of worry, tension, frustration, and dysfunction, gaining some "psychological work space," regaining control of what's happening around you, and getting away from survival living and into problem solving are what *stress management* is all about. And that's *all* it's about. Some writers and "experts" sell stress management as a total lifestyle effort that's the best thing since sliced white bread. That's just absurd. As Abraham Maslow so candidly observed, "When you give a kid a hammer, everything suddenly needs hammering." So many stress and stress-management experts today see debilitating stress lurking under every bush and insist that a total change in the way we live is the only "solution" to the "problem." Frankly, that prescription turns us off.

Stress management is nothing more or less than a tool box of fairly simple-to-learn techniques that can be used to minimize both the pressure of life's big traumas and the escalating annoyances of the everyday "drip, drip, drips." Stress-management tools and techniques are not mysterious or esoteric. They are things you can learn to do to keep the pressure of daily living and selling from putting you off your feed and feet. Things that can help you maximize the chances of being in clear-headed, pro-active, problem-solving, decision-making control of your life and work.

Let's take the case of thirty-four-year-old Jerry Mapes, a hotshot New Orleans real estate salesman. At the age of twenty-four, Jerry forsook junior-high basketball coaching and teaching and, with his uncle's encouragement, went into real estate. At twenty-six, Jerry was licensed, certified, and selling up a storm. Three years later, Jerry had moved up from "moving" two-bedroom, bath-and-a-half, ticky-tacky bungalows to showing fine, New Orleans Garden District, upper-middle-class residential properties. He was beginning to deal in small, commercial properties and medium-sized multi-unit dwellings as well. His income tracked a handsome parallel with the rest of his career.

But at age thirty-four, when Ron Zemke met him, Jerry was seriously considering running away to the farthest bayou, growing a beard, and becoming a hermit. He was willing—almost eager—to toss away a lifestyle most would envy for. . . . He wasn't quite sure *what* for. And that's why he buttonholed Ron in the spring of 1978, after Ron made a presentation to a real estate group. Eventually, Jerry joined a three-day workshop, and, during the course of it, he identified the issues—both on and off the job—that made him want to opt out. He found the carrot-stick treadmill he was on—the uncertainty of income flow, the long hours, nights and weekends devoted to showings—had become the be-all, end-all of his life. He was divorced and found little time for dating or even smelling the proverbial roses. When he had free time, he slept. Jerry was suffering an "existential crisis"—all stressed up and nowhere to go with it. He was tired of fighting and ready to flee.

But, during the workshop, Jerry made new decisions about the amount of income he really wanted to earn. He learned how to worry *productively* in ways that lead to more sales in less time (by cutting *worry* time to a bare minimum). He also learned to become less upset by, and accepting of, the "givens"—things such as the necessity of evening and night work and constantly being in the middle, between buyer and seller in his business. He was able, for the first time, to take time to look at the cost/benefit ratio of weekend work (what he gained versus what he lost socially and interpersonally), so that he could decide on a plan of action. In a sense, he learned that his life and stress were largely products of the decisions he and others had made about his life. Thus, he resolved to take his decision making more seriously.

Jerry was then able to re-evaluate old goals, re-focus and adjust them, and add new goals. The high stress and tension he'd been feeling had acted as a major barrier both to constructive thinking and to taking appropriate action. As Jerry established new priorities, he decided that selling commercial property would free his weekend time for living. He felt the anticipated rewards of the work would outweigh the uneven income flow.

You'll note that nothing was done *to* or *for* Jerry. He did it himself. Just as he did everything connected with selling, from prospecting to closing, by himself, he also changed the stress in his life by himself. We simply shared some ideas with him that he found useful to his own self-changing needs. Jerry drove the car and we provided a readable road map.

Jerry's story is important not only as case study but as a good example of what any highly stressed individual can accomplish with some knowledge, training, guidance, and the right stress-management techniques. Jerry's story is also important because it typifies, in a slightly exaggerated way, the everyday pressures salespeople confront and the stress-management needs of so many people we've met who sell for a living.

Selling is a high-tension occupation. Of all the occupations one might pursue, selling is one of the most "naked." Salespeople succeed or fail, eat or starve, entirely on the sales they make. No excuse is a good excuse for a "no sale." There's no hiding, no glossing over, no rationalizing away failure. It's just too obvious. The salesperson truly stands naked and at the mercy of the stark "sink or swim" criteria.

What are the pressures and events that often precipitate a stress reaction in the professional salesperson? For the novice or would-be professional salesperson, there's the anticipation or fear of failure. Selling is, in many ways, a performing art. Just as the novice actor never really knows what will happen, how he or she will respond when the curtain goes up on a live audience, the beginning salesperson is never completely sure that he or she won't freeze—and fail—when the door is closed and the client says, "You've gotten past my secretary and you've gotten past my assistant. What's so important that you need to see me personally?" Even the best old pro feels that tug of war from time to time. It can motivate, or it can debilitate. But either way, it exacts a price.

In addition, professional salespeople face the possibility of psychological rejections, those "little murders" that the sales process forces the salesperson to confront day after day. One expert in the insurance field has calculated that for every yes an insurance salesperson hears, he or she hears over fifty no's. Another expert has calculated that each sale a life insurance agent makes is the result of five presentations; each presentation is the outcome of ten initial interviews; and each initial interview is the result of ten cold calls.

Small wonder, then that *Training Magazine's* recent national training-needs survey found sales managers complaining that their salespeople are reluctant to make cold calls and that they call on existing accounts too frequently, hesitate to ask for the order, and spend too much time in the office. Just as young children quickly learn to avoid hot stoves, salespeople learn to avoid life's punishing events.

Add to this the distasteful fact that most salespeople are at the mercy of someone's "goodwill" for their livelihood. Of all of us who work for a living, only salespeople are denied the privileges of ill temper, bad days, avoiding people they don't like, and talking back to the rude and crude of the world. It's easy to imagine the day-to-day stress a salesperson experiences. And it's not surprising that the primary reason salespeople give for leaving the business is "I can't take it anymore." What's *it*? Rejection, of course.

Another source of stress for a salesperson stems, ironically, from his or her efforts to improve and become a better salesperson. Every salesperson is painfully aware of the intangible process difference between a sale almost made and a sale almost lost. That same little difference is also the margin of success upon which his or her career rests. Consequently, salespeople continually attend seminars and lectures and read about selling. They're looking for an "edge," any edge, that might help them improve. But the hoped-for result often falls short of expectation; and when they try to resume doing whatever it was that was effective in the first place, they don't know what it was.

Most of us are like that: we're not really conscious of what we do that makes us good. In other words, we're unconscious competents. When we're good, there's no one better. When we're bad, well. . . The trouble, of course, is not knowing what we do that produces good or bad results. John Wannamaker, the great Philadelphia retailer, reportedly shouted out in exasperation, "Half of my advertising is no damn good! The hell of it is, I don't know *which* half." So it is with each of us, and so it is with many, if not most, successful salespeople. When we're really doing our tap dance well, we're too busy reading the audience to watch our footwork.

Too much travel, too many nights on the road, and too much weekend work, all the things so poignantly described in Sam Susser's *The Truth about Selling*, take a toll on family life and bring tension into the home. But even more troublesome than the travel and the other demands of selling that interfere with normal home life is stressful communication. A long day of being nice, glib, and verbally careful with customers can take a toll in at-home communications. And who pays the toll? Generally, an unsuspecting spouse or child, who's comments or questions meet with short, angry responses that close off *all* communication. And, of course, that doesn't play well with anyone. The sales pro ends up feeling just as bad as the spouse, the child, or the kicked cat.

We sincerely believe that sales professionals, by becoming aware of the role stress plays in the selling process and by learning to anticipate and recognize destructive stress, can successfully deal with the fears, rejections, and pressures to perform that send them out in search of ways to get better—or home in a blue funk. We believe, in fact, the stress that often threatens to debilitate and diminish the sales professional's performance, if recognized early on and properly channeled and managed toward positive efforts, can become part of his or her competitive edge.

Stressless Selling offers an approach, a set of techniques, to help you, the sales professional, deal with the stresses engendered in the day-to-day business of making a living selling. *Stressless Selling* doesn't present a new way to establish trust or twenty tricks to better closings. *Stressless Selling* won't replace Napoleon Hill's *Think and Grow Rich* as the best-selling sales book of all time. It won't supersede either Dale Carnegie's *How to Win Friends and Influence People* or Norman Vincent Peale's *Power of Positive Thinking* as favorite inspirational readers for salespeople. But it will show you, the sales professional, specific proven techniques for finding and freeing the energy you need to reach the goals to which you aspire, to gain control of your life space, and to learn to live way beyond the bottom line.

SORTING OUT
THE STRESS MESS:
WHAT'S FACT,
WHAT'S FICTION?

chapter one

all about
stress

STRESS IS . . .

Stress is as common as the common cold—and, in some ways, just as poorly understood. And, contrary to what you might think, stress has been a problem for a long time. Even in ancient Greece, men of letters lamented the emotional toll of the "pace of modern civilized life." Contemporary experts have defined stress as:

- "The wear and tear of life"
- "The inevitable cost of significant achievement"
- "Life events demanding an adaptive response from the organism"
- "The cost of being alive"
- "The spice of life"

3

The definition we prefer was developed at Cornell University Medical College for use in the school's innovative physician stress education program[1]:

We have defined it (stress) as the ordinary and extraordinary pressures of life that confront every person. When the sum of these pressures exceeds a person's ability to cope, the effects may indicate a need for professional help. . . . For each of us, there is a limit to the total pressure we can take at any one time. And when that limit is exceeded, physical and emotional changes occur that may mar our health.

Regardless of who does the defining, there seem to be two common elements in most definitions of stress. The first is that none is very precise about exactly what stress is and does. They all lack the precision and technicality we've come to expect from modern medicine. Interestingly, that very absence of specificity is an honest and essential feature of stress and stress-related maladies. Compare stress with a common, garden-variety broken leg. A broken leg is tangible: the pain is localized, so you know where it hurts and how much; you can touch the injured spot, watch it bruise, and eventually watch and feel it heal. And you have a mental image of how medicine goes about mending a broken leg. Kindly Dr. Brown sets it, puts it in a cast, and, inconvenient as the cast may be for a few weeks, you know the break is healing. A broken leg fits the standard model of "sick" that we all know and have understood since childhood.

But stress isn't like that. It doesn't fit the standard getting-sick-and-getting-well model. For instance, we **need** some stress in our lives: To be alive is to be stressed. Getting married is stressful. Going on a vacation is stressful. Making a call on a new prospect is stressful. Getting out of bed can be stressful! Without that stress, we wouldn't be sharp and alert. The absence of stress, says Dr. Hans Selye, is death.

Even when stress goes beyond our normal tolerance and becomes distracting and destructive, it doesn't act like a disease. It lacks that clear, obviously disabling quality of, say, a broken leg or a case of the measles. Take, for instance, the symptoms of stress: tension headaches, sleep problems, heartbeat irregularities, fatigue, choking sensations, irritability, nervousness, inability to concentrate, indigestion, diarrhea. The problem, of course, is that these symptoms could belong to any number of diseases. And so, like the chameleon behind its protective coloration, stress is often masked or hidden behind its physiological symptoms. It often looks like something else, something that it isn't.

Stress often **resembles** a simple organic disease, but treating the diarrhea or insomnia or migraine headache doesn't eliminate the stress and sometimes even fails to relieve the symptoms. In the medical argot, stress is a **functional**

[1] The Cornell University Medical College program, "The Consequences of Stress: The Medical and Social Implications of Prescribing Tranquilizers," is under the direction of Dr. Theodore Cooper and is funded by a grant from Roche Laboratories. The two-and-one-half year program has reached nearly 10,000 primary-care physicians and psychiatrists.

illness, a condition that impairs like, and looks like, an organic disease—but is not one.

The second common characteristic of any attempt to define stress is the necessity of considering both the physiological and psychological natures of stress. That's not especially comfortable for modern medicine, which tends to treat the body as a machine. That approach is fine for dealing with a broken leg or a bullet wound, but it breaks down when applied to stress. Because stress is a combination of psychological and physiological responses to the ordinary and extraordinary pressures of life, it often looks like something it's not. Some medical people, such as IBM's Dr. Alan McLean, author of **Work Stress**, refer to stress as a psychosomatic, or mentally induced, illness. And, as we'll soon see, psychological subtleties, such as perception of events, interpretation of situations, and understanding of options, **are** extremely important in the management and control of stress. Our **heads** play a critical role both in **becoming stressed** and in **managing stress**. Therefore, since stress can have both psychological and physical origins and symptoms, we must be aware of both the psychological and physical characteristics in order to effectively control the stress responses in our lives.

So here's how we are going to look at stress. Stress is our body's psychological, physical, and chemical **response** to life events that frighten, threaten, excite, confuse, annoy, irritate, invigorate, or endanger us. The specific events or the accumulation of events—let's call them **stressors**—that trigger a **stress response** can be good or bad, happy or sad. And they're fairly individualistic: an event that may cause a friend to sweat profusely and tremble like a leaf may only bore you; the thought of delivering a public address may terrify a college speech student but invigorate a politician.

As we look at various stress reactions, we'll need to be aware of "size" differences. Some stress reactions are quite subtle, so mild that we never notice them. Some responses are painfully obvious—trembling hands, sweating palms, pounding heart, cracking voice. Remember Richard Nixon's shaking voice and sweaty upper lip as he spoke his words of resignation? Even the most rabid Nixon foe couldn't fail to appreciate the stress so clearly displayed in living color (ashen) from coast to coast for all to see.

We'll also need to take a quick look at the physical/medical costs and causes of stress, and we'll need to be aware of the tangled thicket of the illness/stress relationship, the interplay of stress, illness, and chronic disease. We'll emphasize that being stressed can make you ill—and being ill can make you stressed. It's sometimes difficult to tell which piece of the puzzle you're looking at **and** experiencing. Stress, as we've already said, won't fit the broken-leg model of sick and well.

We'll look carefully at the behavioral aspects of stress: how we act toward situations, people, and life in general says much about our individual stress origins. Because stress has such important impacts on our behavior toward ourselves and others, we'll suggest some behavior-change ideas. And, finally, we'll look at stress as a very individualistic problem with individual management needs.

But we won't be offering any one-best-way solutions or approaches to managing stress. Instead, we'll try to show *you* how to analyze the origins and types of stress in your life and give you some guidelines for developing your own special stress-management techniques. Don't expect to find a magic formula for ridding yourself of stress forever and ever. "Happily every after" is only for fairy tales. "Better than it used to be" is the reality of change. But you know that. After all, you sell for a living, and you know that pie in the sky only gets to the plate one slice at a time.

Two Promises to You, the Reader

A lot of nonsense has been written and spoken about stress and stress management. Dozens of unqualified, self-professed "stress experts" have appeared out of the woodwork. Magazines have interviewed any physician, psychologist, and consultant who can pronounce cardiovascular four times without stuttering, and every new business book has a mandatory stress chapter that explains how MBO, interpersonal communications, or whatever the book is really about is a sure cure for stress. By our estimate, half of *everything* we've read about stress in the past few years is either harmless hot air or dangerous misinformation.

So let's make a deal. We won't waste much space trying to "sell" you on the problem and the cure. There will be no apocryphal case studies cited to show you how brilliant we are. Instead, we'll introduce you to a number of people we have worked with and learned from. But *they're* the ones who were suffering from excessive stress, and they're the ones who did the work of learning to manage that stress. We simply supplied them with some how-to information. No one "saves" anyone else. Getting better is a first-person singular job. Nor will we try to scare you with a recitation of ominous statistics in the "1.5 out of every 3.6 people are stress victims" vein. We'll pass along a *few* statistics and the currently held medical opinion about what diseases may be stress-related. And we promise *not* to promise that you'll be taller or wiser or that your athletes foot or acne problem will clear up as a result of learning to better manage the stresses in your life.

We do promise to sort the wheat from the chaff and faithfully report what we—and others—have learned about stress as a social, occupational, and personal problem and what we're all learning about stress in selling and workable stress-management techniques. We won't exaggerate and we won't distort, but we will report what is *actually known* about stress. One more promise. We're all too familiar with experts who write books that "tell you more about penguins than you really want to know about penguins." So, we'll do our best to avoid telling you more about stress and stress management than you really want to know.

People need to understand a little bit about where an idea comes from and how it evolves before they're comfortable with it. A touch of background helps us connect the new idea with things we already know. This "historical" approach has helped us understand stress and stress management—and sort fact from fancy.

Early work on stress came from the medical world. Until quite recently, medical and physiological research treated man and mouse as relatively equivalent organisms—the mouse being the more cooperative of the two for research purposes. This early medical work caused some confusion because it tended to focus on the physical aspects of stress, ignoring the behavioral and mental connections.

But, as we all know, the mind and body work together. And they are inseparably intertwined in the matters of stress and stress management. To clarify, we are going to be talking about *three environments* and the way they work, together and separately, to cause stress. These three environments are: the *external physical environment* (heat, cold, air, light, sound, and the like); the *internal physical environment* (physical systems—blood, digestion, nerves, glands, muscles, drugs, ingested food, age, and condition of organs); and the *internal psychological environment* (thoughts, emotions, experiences, perceptions, knowledge).

In the Beginning

In the late 1800s, Claude Bernard, a French physiologist, theorized and demonstrated that the internal environment of human beings must remain fairly constant if the human being is to exist. Body temperature, blood pressure, chemical composition of body fluids and tissues tend to remain constant regardless of changes occurring around the person. This miracle takes place despite the adverse things we do to our bodies.

Bernard's specific contribution toward understanding stress was to point out and prove that the constancy of this internal milieu was a desirable condition. And when our body's self-regulating system has a "power failure," we can experience illness, disease, and even death. Stress can trigger such a power failure, which knocks the self-regulating system "out of whack."

Round Two: Fight/Flight

Some fifty years later, in the early 1900s, Harvard physiologist Walter B. Cannon coined the term *homeostasis* to describe the power or drive of the body to maintain organic steadiness or equilibrium. Cannon believed that if the body is thrown out of balance and, for some adaptive reason, must move away from homeostasis, or if it is stretched beyond its normal shape or function by an outside force, it almost immediately begins struggling to return to normal. Illness is not just suffering; it is also a fight to bring homeostatic balance to organs and tissue, despite the damage the body may have incurred.

Cannon's best-known contribution to the stress picture is his discovery, around 1909, of a bodily reaction known today as the "fight/flight response." Cannon and colleague Paul Bard noticed that when an animal is repeatedly placed in a *harmful situation*, it develops a sort of "get ready" response. That is, lab animals that have been experimentally shocked, restrained, or in some way harmed, respond quite differently when brought into the lab than do "naive" animals. Cannon and Bard noticed that these "experienced victims" responded in an "integrated physiologic fashion"; the animal's body begins preparing the animal for running or fighting.

Once aware of this *learned response* (our term, not their's), Bard and Cannon began to see almost identical physical symptoms among their human patients. Cannon documented the case of a woman whose body ceased normal digestive functions and who exhibited extremely anxious behavior whenever she visited Boston. The explanation, it turned out, was that the woman's husband often "became uncontrollably drunk" each time he came to the "big city." The day after the anticipated "toot," the woman's anxiety disappeared, and her digestive system resumed normal functioning. (Cannon made no record of the husband's state of "day-after" functioning.)

Cannon and his colleagues then speculated that all of us have a built-in fight/flight response that can be triggered by situations we learn to perceive as threatening. Various theories suggest that the fight/flight response is probably one of the built-in mechanisms that helped our primitive cavemen cousins avoid being "dinner" for stronger and quicker neighbors, such as the saber-toothed tiger. Even today, when we're confronted with a threatening situation—being on a dark street, say, in a strange town at 3 A.M. and facing an unfriendly stranger who has a gun—we're suddenly aware that the fight/flight response is as much a part of our repertoire as it was of our primitive forebears.

The fight/flight response is characterized by coordinated increases in oxygen consumption or metabolism and increases in blood pressure, heart rate, and volume of blood pumped to the skeletal or action muscles. Evidence exists that the blood actually becomes thicker, clotting agents are secreted, and the capillaries and vessels near the skin's surface shut down, as do digestion and digestive juice secretions.

When we're facing a mugger or a touchy high-speed highway incident or when we're preparing and pumping up for an athletic competition, these reactions are helpful to us. But there are also times when these reactions are dysfunctional. One can't, for instance, solve much by becoming fight/flight activated and clobbering or threatening a buyer. Running away from an irate boss doesn't solve much either. And what sense does it make to be aroused for survival in the middle of a five o'clock traffic jam? Civilized humans have learned an alternative to fight/flight. It's called problem solving. But how do we tell our *bodies* that we don't need a full-blown fight/flight response all the time? We can't, completely. So, often when we're being reprimanded by a customer, a cop, a boss, or even a spouse, we find ourselves physiologically aroused and ready to reach for the jawbone of an ass (or the ass's jawbone), but we resist and exercise "civilized control." That, of course, leaves us all stressed up with no place to go. The only clobbering that occurs is the beating our bodies take from the physiological stress of harboring that very natural built-in fight/flight response and resisting it.

Thirty Years of Time-Out

A critical debate raged through the twenties and thirties about the origin of emotions and their relationship to the body and body chemistry. On one side were Cannon, a number of physiologists, and the one or two early behavioral psychologists. On the other side was a group of philosopher/psychologists led by the persuasive and erudite psychologist William James and Danish physiologist Carl Lang. The debate centered around the relationship of emotion, perception, and the biochemistry of fight/flight. The questions debated were essentially these three:

1. Do we "feel" emotions because of changes in bodily chemistry?

2. Or do we have bodily chemistry changes because of the emotions we feel?

3. What is the role of the mind's appraisal of the threat of a particular set of circumstances in emotion and the body's biochemical reactions?

In more basic terms, do we see the bear, run, and then become frightened? Or do we see the bear, become frightened, and then run? Or is none of the above the correct answer?

A Little Guy with a Hole in His Stomach

During the early forties, researchers Stewart Wolf and Harold Wolff "discovered" a man named Tom who was forced, through the circumstances of a freak accident, to live most of his adult life with his stomach open and connected to the surface of his body. Though Wolf and Wolff intended to concentrate on the study of the mechanical actions of Tom's stomach functions, they found that his moods, feelings, and even his thoughts had a significant effect on his stomach function. In one reported example, Wolf and Wolff happened to be working with Tom in their lab twenty-four hours after he'd had a particularly distasteful encounter with a pompous hospital administrator. During preparation for the experiment, Tom began to relate his tale of woe and humiliation of the previous day. As he relived and related the incident, the redness of Tom's stomach lining, the volume of free stomach acid, and the acid secretion all increased. The researchers then made an effort to distract and divert Tom's attention from the unhappy incident. Within thirty minutes, most of the arousal characteristics had reversed themselves. Wolf and Wolff's work with Tom clearly demonstrated that mental, emotional, and behavioral events have as much impact on the body as do drugs, germs, alcohol, and other tangible physical commodities.

Stress Becomes "Legit"

Few of us would even know about the work we've discussed so far if it hadn't been for a single brilliant and dedicated researcher, Dr. Hans Selye.[2] Whether we know it or not, our awareness of stress as a health and happiness issue is due primarily to his work. Born in Vienna in 1907, Selye took training in endocrinology and biochemistry in Prague, Paris, and Rome. He received his M.D. and a Ph.D. in philosophy and science at German University in Prague.

Since 1945, Selye has served as director of the Institute of Experimental Medicine and Surgery at the University of Montreal. At last report, he had written thirty-two books and more than 1,500 technical medical articles. By his own count, he has the world's largest stress library, boasting 110,000 titles. Small wonder he is referred to as *the* dean of stress research.

Early in Selye's medical studies, he became interested in trying to understand exactly what it meant to "be ill." As a student, he noticed that, regardless of the specific disease, illness, injury, or trauma the body suffers, there are a number of common responses.

Later, in his own laboratory, Selye saw that regardless of the damage he imposed on experimental animals, a peculiarly consistent, general pattern, or syndrome, of responses accompanied the specific injury responses. Whether he exposed his lab rats to extremes of heat or cold, excessive x-ray irradiation, physical abuse, prolonged immobility, forced exercise, or traumatic surgery, the same trio of general responses was always present:

- considerable enlargement of the *adrenal cortex*, the outer surface of the adrenal glands;

[2] In 1936, Selye was the first to use the term *stress* to describe the phenomenon he had been studying for almost ten years. In the 1976 revision of his classic 1956 book, *The Stress of Life*, Selye reveals that in the days when he was fighting the battle to make the term stress "stick" to the phenomenon he was studying and writing about, his English was less than perfect. Had he to do it over again, he suggests, he would use the word *stress* to represent the trigger and *strain* the effect. That way, the engineering and medical meanings of stress would be similar. Today, of course, we are stuck with *stressor* as the cue (cause) and *stress* as the result. This lack of parallel linguistic structure between engineering and medical uses of the word *stress* sometimes leads to confusion.

- intensive shrinking of the *thymus*, the *spleen*, and the *lymph nodes*, all of which are related to the cleansing of body fluids; and

- bleeding and ulceration in the *stomach* lining and the *duodenum*, the uppermost part of the intestine.

Selye eventually called this response pattern the *stress syndrome*. Note that Selye worked with and wrote about the body as a machine. Until recently, he took only minor interest in the emotional, cognitive, and voluntary behavioral aspects of stress response. He has considered psychological *stressors* in his work, but he has concentrated on the body costs of being stressed and ignored the psycho-emotional costs.

Further research showed Selye that the body's response to stress or being under stress changes over time. That is, the longer the stress persists, the more likely it is that the body's response to the stress will change. Selye documented a three-step pattern he calls the *General Adaptation Syndrome*.

1. *Alarm Stage.* When the body is initially stressed, it responds with an alarm reaction; it mobilizes. This mobilization is basically the activation of *fight/flight*, though Selye never uses that term. This is also the stage Wolf and Wolff studied in their work with Tom. Selye refers to this stage as "the bodily expression of a general call to arms of the defensive forces of the organism."

2. *The Resistance Stage.* After a persistent and prolonged exposure to the stressor or stressful situation, the body begins to resist its own alarm reaction and, in a sense, acts as if the stressor is no longer present. The body begins regenerating itself: blood returns to a normal density and chemical composition, body weight increases, and adrenalin begins to return to a normal level. The adrenals even begin to store adrenalin again.

3. *The Exhaustion Stage.* If the stress continues too long or if the stress load increases substantially, the body goes on alert again and pumps adrenal gland hormones into the system. This second arousal reaction continues until the defenses are drained and the body ceases to have any adaptive response capability—hence, Seyle's emphasis that stress is a disease of adaptation. "We are just beginning to see that many common diseases are largely due to errors in our adaptive response to stress rather than to direct damage by germs, poisons or life experience," he writes. "In this sense, many nervous and emotional disturbances, high blood pressure, gastric and

duodenal ulcers, and certain types of sexual, allergic, cardiovascular and renal derangements appear to be essentially *diseases of adaptation.*"

If stress continues unabated, the only remaining outcome is death. In a sense, the body becomes its own worst enemy.

Selye points out some important cautions regarding the *general adaptation syndrome*. First, he says that few of us ever reach the exhaustion stage. Those of us who do rarely experience true exhaustion long enough to significantly damage our bodies. Arctic explorers, people trapped in very hostile physical environments, excessively abused P.O.W.s, ruthlessly tortured political prisoners, and a few athletes who attempt unrealistic feats do experience the deep and prolonged exhaustion that leads to irreparable physical damage and death. But in normal life, we tend only to experience exhaustion in mild forms and small, short doses. We do, however, commonly experience the *alarm* and *resistance* stages. Secondly, Selye emphasizes that, even when we do experience the *exhaustion* stage, we are seldom in any immediate danger—unless, of course, we choose not to heed, or can't heed, this built-in warning to slow down.

To find out how the general adaptation syndrome works, let's take a run with George. George is a recreational distance runner. In this scenario, he is about to take part in the "Over-the-Hill-Gang Ten Kilometer Fun Run." First, George warms up by stretching, jogging about, and doing other exercises to "get into it." Although he isn't aware of it, warm-up activities put the body on alert by purposely inducing mild *alarm reaction* and signaling the physical systems that increased activity is coming.

Heart beating quickly, adrenalin pumping into his system, aroused and alert, George hears the gun and sprints off with the pack. During the first mile, he probably runs at an even, regular pace. Once George "gets into the groove," he trots along feeling great, body working at maximum efficiency, leg muscles and cardiovascular system pumping at an even pace. George is experiencing the *resistance* stage.

Eventually, though, he begins to tighten up. His running begins to be more taxing, and he notices himself tiring. This is the onset of the *exhaustion* stage. At this point, George consciously "pulls himself together." His body goes back on alert, and he gets a second wind. Things feel great again—for a short time.

However, George's legs soon begin to feel heavy. Perhaps his stomach cramps. His skin may feel hot and then cold, his heart may seem to be pounding irregularly, and oxygen may be tough to come by. George begins "sucking wind," as the horse trainers say. He is becoming exhausted.

Let's assume George has been training by running two or three miles every other day for the last two months. Suppose also, as is quite likely, that the exhaustion stage hits at about the four-mile post of the race. George probably won't do too much damage to his body by finishing the race. In fact, it may be beneficial to his overall fitness to go ahead and push himself a bit. At worst, he might experience sore legs and a stiff back for a couple days and feel tired the rest of the race day. He might even have a headache the next morning, but that's about all the damage, assuming he is in normal good health.

Suppose, though, that George is under the illusion that one must "face" and "run through" pain. He decides that if a little pain is good for you, a lot will be better. So not only does he finish the original 6.2 miles, but he runs another 10 miles. Chances are pretty good that George is heading for heavy-duty trouble. He could definitely overtax his body's adaptive systems and damage vital organs or tissues.

For a less rigorous example of the general adaptation syndrome in action, take the case of making an important group sales presentation. On the way to the call, you "psych up" by mentally rehearsing your presentation and giving yourself a pep talk. You get to the call, do some relationship building, some scene setting, and then you settle down to work. You rise to your feet and begin your presentation. You feel tingly, alert, conscious of your "upness." Translating back to Selye, you're in the *alarm reaction phase*.

But fifteen minutes into your presentation, you relax your shoulders, your mouth stops being dry, and you feel "in the groove." Of course, you're still alert, still feeling that extra bit of exhilaration that always accompanies the challenge of a tough call, but you definitely feel in control. You've entered the *resistance stage*.

Suppose your presentation lasts another two hours. You're beginning to wear out. And now comes the famous "Any more questions?" phase of the meeting, and some bright guy says, "I'm convinced. Why don't we go pitch my boss?" Of course, his boss has never heard of you or your proposal and thinks that your "gatekeeper"—the joker you mistakenly thought was the decision maker—is a bit of an easy mark for salespeople. Net-net. You have to start all over. But you're tired and operating on only three cylinders. Mr. Boss, of course, has a few questions for you, beginning with, "Now, just why do you think we need *your* help in this matter, Mr. Vendor?" You dig in, find a second wind, and you're off and running—right into the *exhaustion phase*, that is.

If a good night's sleep or a couple days of rest bring you back up to par, you've simply experienced the stress phenomenon. And so what? The problem, of course, arises if the stressful situation continues unabated, and you feel doomed to ever-increasing exhaustion. Say, for example, you've done such a beautiful job with the group sales presentation, surprise and all, that your boss decides you should make *all* the group presentations for the office. Not only that, but he schedules one for every other day for the next month.

Should that happen, you're likely to experience a level and load of stress that can become dysfunctional, and you're potentially headed for the physical problems so well documented by Selye's lifetime of pioneering work. A lifetime of work that has brought him to conclude:

Life is largely a process of adaptation to the circumstances in which we exist. A perennial give-and-take has been going on between one living being and another, ever since the dawn of life in the prehistoric oceans. The secret of health and happiness lies in successful adjustment to the ever-changing conditions on this globe; the penalties for failure in this great process of adaptation are disease and unhappiness.[3]

EQUAL RIGHTS FOR THE PSYCHE: FINDING THE MIND/BODY CONNECTION

The final piece to the stress puzzle is the mind/body link: What role do our emotions, thoughts, and perceptions play in the way we experience and physically respond to stressful situations and events? We have seen that Cannon, Wolf and Wolff, Seyle, and others acknowledged that the mind is an important factor in stress. But as physiologists and medical researchers, they were much more interested in the body as a machine. They tended to view the mind as a picture window through which impressions and sensations freely flowed, much the way sensations of heat and cold flow from the skin.

The role of the mind as a data processor and interpreter of events seemed to be of minor importance to them. This attitude closely paralleled the attitude most medical practitioners once held toward the concept of psychosomatic, or mentally induced, physical illnesses. Certainly, common speech had long been peppered with expressions hinting at the mind/body connection. Armies "traveled on their stomachs," people were able to "worry themselves sick," anger was credited with the ability to "stir the blood," and joy, the power to "make one weep." Romantic poets have even blamed love for maladies ranging from heart palpitations to fever, from goose bumps to intense pain.

Obviously, we all have an intuitive grasp of the relationship between health, physical well-being, thoughts, and emotions. But the scientific study of this intuition is quite another matter and one of only passing interest to the medical world for many years.

One of the earliest efforts to systematically study the relationship of mental stress to bodily response was conducted by Dr. Jon Broda, a Czech scientist. In one of Broda's experiments, several young adults were placed in a room and instructed to solve a series of arithmetic problems in their heads and report the answers to Broda's assistants. The assistants, however, were instructed to chastise the subjects for their slowness in solving their problems and otherwise harass them about their performance.

Broda measured the subjects' blood pressure and took blood samples immediately before and after the experimental harassing. At the end of the ex-

---

[3]Selye, Hans, *The Stress of Life* (rev. ed.). New York: McGraw-Hill, 1976 (pp. xv-xvi).

periment, he found that blood pressure had risen significantly and the volume of blood circulating increased noticeably; analysis of the pre-post blood samples revealed much higher concentrations of adrenalin and other arousal hormones. Here, then, was solid evidence of the mind/body link, as well as evidence that job or task stress can be physically dysfunctional.

The next major event in the development of the mind/body link occurred during the Second World War. Two army air force psychiatrists, Drs. Roy Grinker and John Spiegel, made careful and detailed observations of hundreds of young combat pilots. Their observations (published in 1945 in book form as **Men under Stress**) contributed significantly to the understanding of the mind/body link in stress. Key among their findings were the high degree of individuality they observed in stress responses and the progressive nature of the stress reaction.

While previous medical stress research had focused on finding predictable patterns of physiologic stress response, Grinker and Spiegel found that the specific symptoms an individual manifests often tend to be related to personality and early life experiences. According to their observation, a flyer who had lung trouble as a child, for instance, might be expected to develop lung trouble when under the severe, prolonged stress of combat.

Whether that response is related to a predisposing physical weakness of the lungs or is simply a learned "illness pattern" the individual is familiar with and uses to express stress is unclear but intriguing. By analogy, most child psychologists—and parents—are familiar with the missing-tonsils syndrome. A youngster who has received considerable attention, sympathy, love, and chocolate ice cream before and after a tonsilectomy will occasionally develop a sore throat and need attention and chocolate ice cream weeks or months after the tonsils are gone and the scar tissue has healed. The birth of a sibling and the looming threat of an upcoming spelling test have both been known to occasion the onset of such mysterious sore throats. The point is that, under stress, any of us may return to an old illness to "express" or "exhibit" the distress we are feeling. But whether the illness is organic or functional doesn't matter. Either way, it's *real*, not imaginary.

Grinker and Spiegel's long-term, detailed personal observations of human beings who lived with the interminable stress of war highlighted, for the first time, the mix of psychological and physical stress reactions humans can experience. Typical of their narrative is this particularly gripping description of the variety of stress reactions they observed:

> **The unending strain eventually produces distress signals affecting any part of the mind or body. Enthusiasm and eagerness easily give way to a great weariness of battle, which is then endured because there is no way out. Transient fears turn into permanent feelings of apprehension. Anxiety may be related for a time only to a reaction limited to the most dangerous moments over the target, but it has a tendency to**

spread until it is continuous or is stimulated by only trivial sounds. Good muscular coordination is replaced by uncontrolled tremors, jerky manipulations and tension. Constant tension leads further to restlessness, which is never satisfied by activity and is intolerant of repose. Sleep dwindles and may give way altogether to insomnia punctuated by fitful nightmares. Appetite is noticeably reduced, and gastric difficulties may appear. Although air sickness is rare, nausea and vomiting after meals, especially breakfast, are fairly common, as is functional diarrhea. . . . With the growing lack of control over the mental and physical reactions come a grouchiness and irritability that interfere with good relations among men. Some give way easily, and others are always in a quarrel or argument. Others become depressed and seclusive, and stay away from their friends to avoid dissension, or because they feel ashamed. Thinking and behavior may become seriously altered. Forgetfulness, preoccupation, or constant brooding over loss of friends in combat experiences destroy purposeful activity. The behavior of the men may become not only anti-social, but completely inappropriate and bizarre.

Their work, and subsequent work by psychologists and psychiatrists in Veterans Administration hospitals, has been influential in establishing psychological disabilities as legitimate illnesses. Without this precedent, it is doubtful that topics such as stress could be discussed and dealt with as openly and honestly as they are today.

After we discuss the following two research events, we will have covered the waterfront of what we need to know to understand the psychological effects of stress in the selling process. One of these studies concerns the effect of cognition (thinking) on stress and one concerns behavior. Both arenas—thoughts and behavior—have significant impact on the origins and management of stress.

In the early 1960s, psychologists Stanley Schachter and Jerome Singer suggested that the way we respond to physiological arousal is, in a large part, determined by what we think and believe about the situation and the way other people behave in the same situation. One of their experiments clarifies this supposition. Schachter and Singer injected a group of students with a solution the students were led to believe was a vitamin shot. The injections were, in fact, adrenalin. Some students were told the vitamin shots would cause, as side effects, heart palpitations and noticeable tremors, both of which are common side effects of adrenalin. Others were told that they would experience itching and headaches, neither of which is an adrenalin side effect. Still others were told that the bogus vitamin shots would have *no* side effects.

To complicate matters, the researchers asked each student to sit in a waiting room under the pretext that he or she would shortly be given a vision test. During the wait, each student was joined in the waiting room by a "stooge," a confederate of the researchers, who acted either *very angry* or *silly and giddy*. Part of the time, the stooge laughed and danced around the room; the rest of the time, the culprit stalked about and finally made an angry display of tearing up a questionnaire he or she had been filling out.

After all the shots and stomping and dancing, some important results were apparent. First, Schachter and Singer found that those students who *had not been told* to expect side effects from the shots, who had no way to explain the *real* physiological effects they experienced, described their own feelings in a way that reflected the stooge's behavior. That is, students who had the shots but who hadn't been told what feelings to expect as a side effect reported feeling *angry*, if they were in the waiting room with an *angry-acting stooge*. Those who had been in the waiting room with a *happy-acting stooge* reported feeling *happy*. In other words, the students who had no information, no set way to think about and explain *what* they were feeling and *why* they were feeling it, tended to attribute the way they felt and acted to the influence of the stooge, regardless of *how* the stooge behaved. Students who were *told* what to expect, in the way of physiological side effects and feelings, were more likely to feel what they were led to expect and weren't very likely to be influenced by the stooge.

Schachter and Singer concluded that the emotions we feel are a product of *both* our physiological state *and* the way we learn to interpret that physiological state. Translating that into the language of *stress*, how we respond to a *stressor* depends upon more than just the changes that occur in our body. The way we perceive, interpret, and have learned to *think about* those changes is also very important.

The practical point here is that we can be inadvertently "infected" by other people's stress. We are all, as Schachter and Singer demonstrated, very suggestible. Simply observing the behavior of others can strongly influence *our* behavior and emotions. We can be inadvertently stressed by being around stressed people. If two people are walking around the office at 9:00 A.M. wringing their hands over the news that the next sales manager is the company's answer to Simon Legree, they will have the entire office polluted with anxiety before lunch. And what shape do you suppose anyone from *that* office will be in for making a 2 P.M. call on a prospect?

Schachter was satisfied to suggest that *first* we are aroused, and then, depending on what's going on in our heads or in the environment around us, we interpret the situation—and our feelings—as happy, sad, threatening, or benign. Our final character in this cast, Dr. Richard Lazarus, was convinced that emotional reaction and bodily arousal *follow* our perception and appraisal of a situation. He started with the simple observation that a person who gets cut while peeling a potato or whittling a whistle has a very different bodily response than someone on an operating table whose chest is cut open for heart surgery. In the case of the cut finger, there's immediate body arousal. In the case of the anesthetized heart-surgery patient, there's no alarm reaction, no adaptation stage, no stress response at all.

Lazarus argued that consciousness and interpretation are critical to stress. Suppose you are walking through the park and an ocelot springs out of the bushes and pounces on a person not twenty yards from you. It doesn't take much imagination to picture yourself running away, heart pounding, limbs trembling, mouth dry, and pants wet. Now picture yourself in your living room watching Marlin Perkins wrestle with a Bengal tiger, or imagine yourself on a zoo walkway, passing a cage with a Bengal tiger in it. It isn't hard to guess at the difference in your responses. A real ocelot really attacking someone in a real park in front of your eyes would probably rate a fifteen on a stress scale of one to ten! Watching Marlin Perkins do his deed with a 1,500 pound tiger on the tube may have a stress value of three or four. Walking past the tiger cage in the zoo may barely rate a two.

Lazarus and Alfert, in a particularly graphic experiment, tested the role of thoughts and interpretation of situations in stress by showing a film that depicted adolescent circumcision rites of a primitive tribe to three groups of college students. The students were "wired up" so their heartbeat rates and galvanic skin response (GSR) levels could be measured while viewing the film. One group was shown the film with no sound track. A second group, which saw the film with a sound track, was told that the people in the film were actors and that no one was being hurt. A third group not only heard the disclaimer on the sound track but was told, before seeing the film, that the people were actors and the action bogus.

As you might expect, the third group, those who were told what they would be seeing, who were told what to expect and think before viewing the film and again during the film, showed the least change in heartbeat rate and GSR.[4] All the groups reacted to the first incident of circumcision on the film, but the third group recovered and returned to normal quickly. By the end of the film, this group was quite relaxed. The other two groups continued to be shocked by the incidents. The group seeing the no-sound-track version reacted the most and was the only group that did not return to a lowered stress level by the end of the film.

Emotions, argued Lazarus and colleagues, play a primary role in the length and strength of the stress experience. And emotions are very much related to the interpretation of events by the individual.

Situation. You're making a third call on a prospect. You've been sharing information and acting as counselor to the prospect in hopes that this value-added effort will make the difference you need to beat out the lower-priced competition. But Mr. Prospect has other ideas: "Sam, I can't thank you enough for all the help you've given me and my staff in getting this program organized and moving in the

[4]GSR or Galvanic Skin Response is a measure of how well the skin conducts electricity. When we perspire, we conduct more current. GSR is often used in lie-detection equipment.

right direction. Unfortunately, *my* boss is a price buyer. I *know* you have better quality, but he could care less. I'm sorry, but that's the way it is."

Sam "A" might react this way:

Interpretation. He thinks: "I'm a failure. I didn't get to the right people, and I didn't make the right moves on Prospect's boss. Boy, did I screw that one up. I'm just a washout."

Immediate Response. Depressed, feels a sense of loss, a little panic, is angry at himself

Long-term Response. Sulking, withdrawn, feels continually tired, wants to hide from everyone

But there are alternative scenarios. Sam "B" might react this way:

Interpretation. He thinks: "You S.O.B. I'll fix you for this. What a louse you are!

Immediate Response. Ears burn, stomach churns, shouts at Prospect, slams doors, stalks out, throws things

Long-term Response. Writes scathing letters to Prospect and Prospect's boss; calls successful bidder and accuses him of duplicity with Prospect; ulcers, hypertension, bad relations with Prospect's company

Sam "C" might react still another way:

Interpretation. He thinks: "Aw nuts! Well, I did the best I could. That's the situation. Maybe I can get a referred lead out of this anyway."

Immediate Response. Understanding of limitations of the situation; disappointment; conciliatory; effort made to "keep door open"

Long-term Response. Follows up later on referred lead aspect; able to forget about incident and go on to greener pastures

Sam "A," Sam "B," and Sam "C" are all reacting to the same situation. But each is responding in accordance with his psychological make-up and in concert with the way that make-up disposes each to interpret the situation and events.

There's another important implication to Lazarus' research. If our emotional response to situations is pretty much governed by how we perceive and interpret and think, we aren't helpless in the face of stress. How we think, perceive, and interpret is under our own control—or can be. That means we can control our stress response. And *that's* a pretty positive message.

Pulling the Mind/Body Connection Together

Schachter, Lazarus, and others have indirectly told us quite a lot about stress in selling. We think it's appropriate to synthesize their findings into a simple three-step model to explain the process and dynamics of becoming stressed.

Step 1: Something Happens

To start the "becoming stressed" process, something must act as a stress cue or trigger. This something, this *potential* stressor, can be a thought or image that originates in your own mind, it can be the words or actions of others, or it can simply be a situation, something that just happens. We refer to these as:

M — Myself — your own thoughts, ideas, and images
O — Others — the actions, words, and emotions of other people
S — Situation — things that just happen around you but are somewhat removed from you, like a traffic jam

Let's suppose we have total access to the thoughts, actions, reactions, and emotions of one Arthur Browne, a sales rep for Amalgamated Industries. It's Tuesday the 14th, the day Art has set aside to make a Green Widget proposal to Ann Chandler, the purchasing agent for Basic Gears, Inc. His game plan is to leave the office at 9:15 A.M.; get to Basic Gears at 9:45 A.M.; meet with Chandler from 10:00 A.M. till 10:30, as scheduled; drive back to the office; and, about lunch time, start announcing to the world that he has a signed on the dotted line a contract with Basic Gears, Inc., for 200,000 Amalgamated Green Widgets. That's his plan. But, as with many plans, the story turns out better on paper than in reality.

Let's look at the **Step 1** part of the tragedy that is about to become Arthur's day. Suppose that on the way to the office, Art begins to think about his coming call on Chandler. He remembers how rude she can be with sales-people. And how she hates it when you're late for an appointment. And how *really* tough she is to deal with when she had a disagreement with spouse, peer, or staff. That thinking is a *potential stress cue* generated solely from Art's MYSELF (M).

Let's suppose Art sidesteps the Myself trap, gets to the office, and zips around collating the last copies of the proposal, getting ready for the Chandler meeting. The boss spies Art and comes charging out of his office, waving a copy of the Chandler proposal, breathing fire, and bellowing, "What d'ya think you're doing with this proposal? I *told* you we want to upgrade Basic to Yellow Widgets this year. Change the proposal—NOW!" *A potential stress cue* originating from OTHERS (O) has just entered our hero's purview.

Let's give Art an A+ in flexibility and suppose that he has sidestepped both the M and O stress cue land mines and is now driving down Highway 94 toward Basic Gears world headquarters. Suddenly a semi-truck loaded with live turkeys on the way to the local processing plant jackknifes thirty yards in front of Arthur's car. It's flapping wings, sliding cars, and pandemonium all over the Interstate. Art slams on the brakes, the car swerves, he almost loses it in a skid, and comes to a stop mere feet from the overturned flatbed. Now Art's a definite candidate for an (S) or SITUATIONAL *stress cue*.

You undoubtedly noticed that we are calling all of these hypothetical happenings *possible or potential* stressors. That's because M's, O's and S's don't automatically act as stressors. A potential stressor or stress cue only becomes a stressor as a result of Step 2.

Step 2: The Mental Interpretation/ Body Reaction Phase

Interpretation. How the mind evaluates events, how we perceive and interpret the threat potential of all the M's, O's and S's we encounter day after day, determines to a large extent our stress reactions to these events. The things that happen to us—and to our friend Arthur—are only potential stressors or stress cues until we think about them and interpret their meaning and personal significance.

If Arthur thinks about Ms. Chandler's nasty behavior toward salespeople and tells himself, "Yeah, she's a tough one all right, but they're the ones I *really* like to sell," he is using Chandler's potential behavior toward him as a cue for positive behavior, not for a negative stress response.

If, however, he goes into the restroom at Basic Gears, straightens his tie, looks in the mirror, and says to himself, "Well, big fella, it's you and me against Chandler and, *personally*, I think we're gonna get clobbered," then Arthur is setting up the conditions for his thoughts, or "MYSELF" (M) *stress cues*, to become stressors.

The same logic holds for the boss's bellowing and the highway accident. If Arthur interprets the turned-over truck of turkeys as the funniest highway accident story of the year, it's much less likely that a high-stress situation will ensue. Though Art will be fight/flight aroused by the accident, the response will be over sooner than if Arthur interprets the accident as death narrowly avoided and then lets that thought run rampant through his mind for hours.

A caution: Sometimes the interpretation of an M-O-S event is so fast we scarcely notice that we're thinking about it. In truth, many interpretations are so ingrained and long-standing that they are basically conditioned responses.

Body Reaction. As you already know, the body's first response to threatening events, be they M's, O's, or S's, is the marshaling of the primitive fight/flight response Bernard, Cannon, Selye, and others investigated so thoroughly. Art's thoughts about Chandler, the boss's behavior, and the brush with death on the freeway, once interpreted as threatening, fire the fight/flight response. And, as we learned from the medical researchers, especially Selye, prolonged arousal—regardless of its magnitude—leads to Step 3, the stress response.

Step 3:
Stress Shows Up
The research we've discussed so far suggests that people respond to continuous or intense activation in one or more of three ways:

- Through our bodies   B
- With our thoughts   T
- Through our actions   A

Depending on the form they take, these reactions can, in fact, be stress reducing and·dispel the negative tension. They can, however, rev you up even further and act as cues for producing additional negative stress. As Lazarus showed with the students watching the circumcision-rites film, the longer some stress cues last, the more the emotional reaction and the higher the stress and tension become. But, as he also showed in the same experiment, the right amount and kind of information can act to dampen and control—and even eliminate—the stress response.

Now, let's check in on poor Arthur to see how he looks, feels, and sounds after that onslaught of M's, O's, and S's. Somehow, despite all the obstacles we've thrown in his path, Art has made his way to the headquarters of Basic Gears International and is seated in Ms. Chandler's office, stressed up to the gills. "Wired" as he is, Art can react in any one, or *all*, of the three ways we discussed—B., T., or A.

One possible effect—or stress response—is that Art's *body* will be telegraphing his "revved up" state. Sweaty palms, cotton mouth, jittery mannerisms are all possible bodily responses that Arthur may manifest for the world—and Chandler—to see.

The second possible stress response, the almost invisible one, is what's taking place in Art's mind—in other words, his *thoughts*. He may sit there "listening" to Chandler, but his mind is focused miles away. He could be ruminating over the near-miss on the highway or brooding about the boss's autocratic behavior. Regardless of which he does, he will surely miss the subleties of Chandler's part of the discussion. He will probably be so "into his own head" that he will completely miss buying signals he would ordinarily pick up in a flash.

We know one salesman who was going through a difficult divorce. He reported that, even in the presence of an important customer, his mind was constantly filled with "Janey, Janey, *why* are you doing this to me?" and "I'm blowing this sale, Janey, and it's all your fault. Why can't I concentrate?" At one point, he even caught himself discussing his marital consternations with prospects. Though extreme, the occurrence of thoughts that are irrelevant and detrimental to the task at hand are just as common as maladaptive somatic or body symptoms.

The third possible stress response is an *action* or behavioral outcome. An *action* stress response could be as simple as rapid speech or telegraphic sentences or as complex as becoming suddenly accident-prone, stumbling over lint on the carpet, kicking over the presentation easel, dropping handout materials in the parking lot, or spilling coffee on the client's desk. And, of course, the worst case of all would be the one wherein Art, hearing his customer suggest that yellow widgets cost too much, flies off the handle and gives the buyer a tongue lashing.

What are the effects on the sale? Sometimes, when the stress is low level and the customer's need for the product or service high, no harm is done. The buyer may have a passing thought about Art's odd behavior but that's all. At other times, the bumblings of a highly stressed salesperson can snatch defeat from the very jaws of victory. At the extreme, an irreparable breach can develop between buyer and seller.

The three-step process is illustrated on page 24.

Step 4: The Sometimes Step

There is a possible fourth step in the becoming-stressed process. Sometimes a stress response "boomerangs" and acts as a *cue* for yet another stress response. This negative boomerang effect sets up a spiral or stress chain. Each stress response becomes a *stress cue*, forging the next link in the stress chain. Graphically, this violence-begets-violence cycle looks like this:

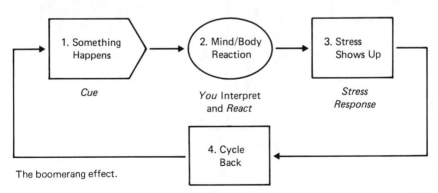

The boomerang effect.

23

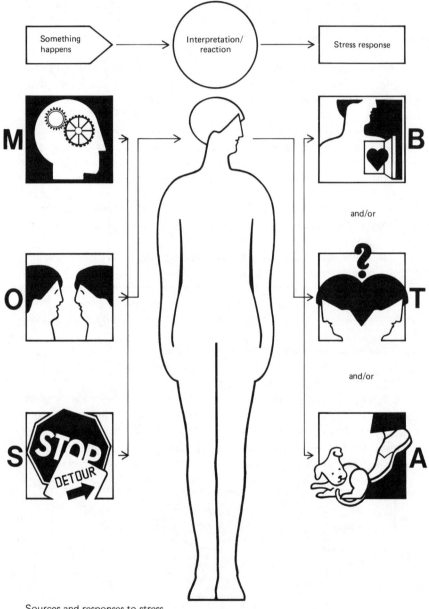

Sources and responses to stress.

Let's raise the curtain on the final act of our melodrama and watch the *stress cycle* destroy poor Arthur's relationship with his customer. As the scene opens, Art is going into the meeting with Chandler, highly stressed, a little shaky, and not completely in control of his concentration skills. How could he be? His mind keeps recycling thoughts about how Chandler hates salesmen, how the boss made him change the proposal from green widgets to yellow widgets at the last minute, and how Chandler is going to toss him out the door on his behind.

Good old Chandler knows her lines and plays her part well. She doesn't go for the proposal and gives Arthur a lecture about being on time and the value of an aesthetically pleasing proposal. Finally, she tells him not to come back until he's ready to make a reasonable proposal for green, not yellow, widgets. Arthur leaves the Basic Gears offices with his heart beating in his throat, extremely upset by both the outcome of the interview and the prospect of being chewed out again by his boss. On the way back to the home office, Arthur gets stuck in a traffic tie-up. Result? Art now has a whole *new* set of stress cues: the dressing down from Chandler, the mental image of the dressing down that the boss is surely going to deliver, and the traffic jam. The net result is more boomerang and more *stress response*. This little melodrama, wherein a *stress response* becomes a *stress cue* and leads to even more stress for Arthur, illustrates the classic *stress cycle*. Not uncommon and not easy to avoid.

Drip, Drip, Drip
Versus Crash, Boom, Bang

We talked earlier about two kinds of stress situations. One is the stress event situation, wherein something clearly happens that triggers the three-step process: *stress cue → interpretation/reaction → stress response*. That's what we just detailed, using poor old hypothetical Arthur as the goat.

We also mentioned the slow seeping or "drip, drip" kind of stress. The major difference between the two situations is that the "little murders," or "drips," accumulate slowly until a noticeable *stress response* takes place. Before there is an observable stress response, however, the *stress cue*, as well as the *interpretation/reaction* part of the system, is in effect. There definitely are both psychological and physiological events occurring. They are, however, only *slightly* above and beyond the normal pressures and responses of living, so there is no obvious or observable *stress response*. After a period of continued "insult," they eventually lead to a stress response that others can notice or that dramatically interferes with performance.

Look at it this way: 1 or 2 or 30 or 100 drops of water hitting the same spot on a marble slab make no noticeable impact; but keep that dripping up until 10,000 or 100,000 or 1 million drops have dripped, and there'll be a hole in the marble. Drip, drip stress acts the same way. We can all shrug off a slightly surly waiter or waitress, weather an occasional abrasive remark by a colleague or loved one, and not get too bent out of shape when we step in a puddle on the way to an important meeting. It is only when these insults, inconveniences, and nasty little breaks go on over a long enough period of time that they finally take their toll and trigger the full *cue → interpretation/reaction → response-cycle back* process.

GETTING TO THE PUNCH LINE

We promised not to tell you more about stress than you wanted or needed to know.[5] We suspect that we're pretty close to that threshold, so it's time to compress all this information about the general psychological, physiological, and behavioral aspects of stress and get to the punch line. The summary we use to keep ourselves straight should be helpful to you. For us, five statements seem to do the trick for remembering the most essential facts about stress.

1. *Stress is inescapable.*

    Everyone experiences stress. The total absence of stress has a technical, medical term—death. Stress is a product of living and striving.

    Too little stress can be as harmful or aggravating as too much. Many of us rely on hobbies and recreation to add stress to our lives. Think of sky divers!

    Some people are actually stress seekers who look for risk, excitement, danger, and the resultant stress in everything they do. Athletes, circus performers, race drivers, stock brokers, and sales managers are high among those who go out of their way to "look for trouble."

2. *Stress is personal.*

    Stresses that upset one person may please another.

    How any one person reacts to stress depends upon a number of social, hereditary, and learned factors.

    We all have different stress-tolerance levels. Some of us can handle more stress than others. Regardless of where you start, your personal stress tolerance can be increased by practice.

3. *Stress is circular or cyclic.*

    Once stress starts, it has a tendency to grow and carry on. It has real momentum. But it isn't a perpetual-motion machine; it just feeds on itself.

[5]For those of you who have an interest in knowing more about the medical aspects of stress, Appendix A in the back of the book contains answers to the ten questions we are asked most frequently about stress and health issues.

Being stressed and tense can lead to, say, hollering at a client or coworkers. The hollering can lead to self-depreciation and devaluation, thus acting not as just an *outcome* but as a *cue* to beat yourself up, adding fuel to the stress fire.

4. *Stress can dramatically influence behavior.*

A positively stressed athlete runs faster, jumps higher, and endures longer during competition than he or she might during practice.

A positively stressed salesperson is alert, confident, and able to solve client problems creatively.

A negatively stressed athlete panics and uses the energy needed for performance in such nonproductive activities as worry, anger, and raging self-doubt.

The negatively stressed salesperson is touchy; blows up at friends, family, and buyers; gives up on tough cases; asks wrong questions; doesn't "hear" answers; fails to read client feedback; and, generally, blocks the use of the sales skill and knowledge he or she already possesses.

5. *Stress can be an asset or a liability.*

Stress in the right amounts and properly managed can motivate, increase good feelings about one's self, and prime you for a "good performance" with a prospect or client.

Stress that's too intense, lasts too long, and goes unmanaged can debilitate. Negative stress can precipitate bodily disorders, worry, anger, and self-doubt. As a precipitator of bodily disorder, it can lead to ulcers, hypertension, and heart disease. As a precipitator of negative thoughts and attitudes, it can shut down creativity, interfere with problem solving, and lead to a negative self-concept and, eventually, withdrawal from selling altogether.

A construction foreman attending a stress-management workshop summarized the stress-balancing act beautifully. "I get it," he observed after hearing the "stress and you" story. "It's like when we build a suspension bridge. If the wires that support the bed are stretched too tight, they snap and the bridge falls down. If the wires are too loose, they don't support anything and it falls down. The trick is to get the tension just right. Then you've got a bridge."

To get from where you are to where you want to be sometimes requires a bridge—a bridge of good performance and positive action. When the tension is just right, that bridge between you and your clients, you and your goals, and you and your loved ones is secure, the traffic flows, and you reach those things you want on the other side you work so hard to reach. It's all in how you string the wires.

chapter two

identifying the stressors in professional selling

Up to this point, we have been occupied with giving you a clear and concise picture of what stress is, where it comes from, and how it affects you—in general. Becoming aware of just what the stress problem is and what you can expect when stress mounts up is an important first step in gaining control of the stress in your life. Defining the problem is almost always the hardest part of any problem-solving effort. Now it's time to zero in on the special, unique problems of stress in *selling*.

In the previous chapter, we quoted and cited twenty or so experts on the medical and psychological aspects of stress. From here on, *you* are the expert. Most of the testimony in this chapter comes from you and your colleagues who sell for a living. It contains things you and others have told us about stress during workshops, on questionnaires and tests, in focus groups, and one-to-one in less formal settings. It also contains our insights into stress in selling that we gained from traveling with you, making sales calls with you, and watching and listening as you went about the business of being a professional salesperson.

If we've done our job, you will see your reflection in this chapter. The ideas, the self-tests, and the prose are feedback—*to you, from you, about you*—filtered through us. As we wrote the following chapters, our goal was, plainly and simply, to "stand in your shoes," "discover your needs," and "hit your hot button"—in other words, to do those things that you have shown us are important when one person attempts to communicate effectively with another.

COMPARED TO WHOM?

Fact: Professional selling is *not* the most stressful occupation. Health-care professionals, air-traffic controllers, accountants, big city police, and, believe it or not, waiters and waitresses all tend to report more on-job stress than do salespeople. So, although there are times when it may not feel like it to you, there are a few tougher, or at least more *stressful*, ways to make a living than selling. *But* the stresses and stressors of selling are unique and different from those of other occupations. In some ways, selling, we believe, has a more detrimental *long-term* effect than all but one or two extremely stressful occupations.

In a survey of 2,800 dentists, conducted in conjunction with *Dental Economics* magazine, for example, we found that dentists ranked "*Patients experiencing pain or discomfort*" as the situation most likely to arouse emotional and physical stress in the dentists themselves. Only slightly less stress-inducing to these same dentists was having a patient in the chair who squirms, spits, and moves his or her tongue about while they, the dentists, are trying to work in the patient's mouth. In other words, dentists report that they are *most stressed* when their patients are in pain or are behaving in a manner that is likely to cause the dentist to cause the patient avoidable pain. So all those jokes about dentists and pain aside, your dentist is as concerned about you experiencing pain as you are.

Obviously, the stressors in selling would be—and are—totally different than those of dentistry. In a study of 375 Million Dollar Round Table (MDRT) insurance salespeople,[1] we found that, out of fifteen different situations, the event most likely to cause these crème de la crème insurance sales pros to feel stressed is "*Losing an old and valued client*." Our MDRT sample ranked this situation as *the* number one stressor they encounter, and they did so 20 percent more frequently than they did their number two stressor, "*Having no active prospects*." One MDRT insurance agent explained to us the significance of losing an old client this way:

> **Look, the goal in life insurance selling is to have a lot of policies in force. That's your income base. It's like coupon clipping or drawing**

[1] The surveys were filled out by MDRT members at their 1979 national convention in Chicago. The data were subsequently published in *Round the Table* Magazine. The article in its entirety appears in Appendix B.